D1401147

THE CASE OF
The Flesh-Eating Bacteria

Michelle Faulk, PhD

Enslow Publishers, Inc.
40 Industrial Road
Box 398
Berkeley Heights, NJ 07922
USA
http://www.enslow.com

Library of Congress Cataloging-in-Publication Data

Faulk, Michelle

   The case of the flesh-eating bacteria : Annie Biotica solves skin disease crimes / by Michelle
     Faulk.
     p. cm. — (Body system disease investigations)
   Includes bibliographical references and index.
   Summary: "Learn about different diseases that affect the skin, such as measles and the chicken
     pox"— Provided by publisher.
   ISBN 978-0-7660-3945-2 (alk. paper)
   1. Skin—Infections—Juvenile literature. 2. Virus diseases—Juvenile literature. I. Title.
   RL201.F38 2013
   616.5'2—dc23   2011023985

Printed in China
062012 Leo Paper Group, Heshan City, Guangdong, China

10 9 8 7 6 5 4 3 2 1

Future editions:
Paperback ISBN 978-1-4644-0224-1
ePUB ISBN 978-1-4645-1138-7
PDF ISBN 978-1-4646-1138-4

To Our Readers: We have done our best to make sure all Internet Addresses in this book were
active and appropriate when we went to press. However, the author and the publisher have no
control over and assume no liability for the material available on those Internet sites or on other
Web sites they may link to. Any comments or suggestions can be sent by e-mail to comments@
enslow.com or to the address on the back cover.

Illustration Credits: CDC, p. 24 (top); CDC: Cynthia S. Goldsmith; William Bellini, Ph.D., pp. 34
(left), 36 (bottom), Dr. Lucille K. Georg, p. 23; Illustrations by Jeff Weigel (www.jeffweigel.com), pp.
1, 3, 5, 8, 13, 15, 19, 21, 27, 30, 31, 33, 37, 38, 39, 40, 42, 46, 47; © Nucleus Medical Art, Inc/Phototake,
p. 15; Photo Researchers, Inc.: AMI IMAGES, pp. 29 (top), 31, ANTONIA REEVE, p. 29 (bottom),
CNRI, pp. 17, 19, Dr. Lucille K. George, p. 42, Dr. M.A. Ansary, p. 33 (bottom), Dr. P. Marazzi, pp. 33
(top), 34 (right), 40, Hybrid Medical Animation, pp. 22, 24 (bottom), PHANIE, p. 18, Scott Camazine,
p. 21 (bottom); Shutterstock.com, pp. 6, 7, 11, 12 (top), 14, 16, 21 (top), 25, 27, 28, 29 (middle), 30, 35,
36 (top), 38, background images, check marks, color blasts, magnifying glasses, question marks;
Used with permission from HMP Communications, pp. 9, 12 (bottom).

Cover Illustration: Illustrations by Jeff Weigel (www.jeffweigel.com)

Contents

My name is **Agent Annie Biotica**. I am a Disease Scene Investigator with the Major Health Crimes Unit. My job is to keep people safe from the troublemaker germs out there. How do I do it? I use logic and the scientific method. I gather clues from health crime scenes. I identify microbe suspects. I gather evidence. If all goes well, I get justice for the victims by curing them. Sometimes all doesn't go well. These are some of my stories.

Annie Biotica

The Human Skin

The skin is the largest organ in the body. It is the first defense in fighting disease. Skin surrounds and protects our soft and fragile internal organs.

The skin has two main layers. The outer layer is the epidermis, with many layers of tightly packed cells. The epidermis is thickest in the palms, fingers, toes, and soles. It is thinnest at the eyelids. New cells are born at the bottom layer. Each new cell pushes the ones above farther up. As the cells rise they accumulate a protein called keratin. Keratin makes skin cells tough and waterproof. As the cells move up and away from nourishing blood vessels they slowly die. The cells fall off when they reach the outside world.

Underneath the epidermis is the dermis. The dermis is thick and contains many interesting things. Collagen fibers make the skin strong. Elastin fibers allow the skin to stretch. Sweat glands ooze sweat onto the surface of the skin. Sweat makes the skin an unfriendly place for disease-causing microbes to spend time. Sebaceous glands secrete oil. This oil contains chemicals that kill many microbes. Nerves and the roots of our hairs are also found in the dermis.

Under these skin layers is tissue that connects the skin to the body. This area is the hypodermis. It has a lot of fatty tissue that acts as a cushion around our body. It also keeps us warm.

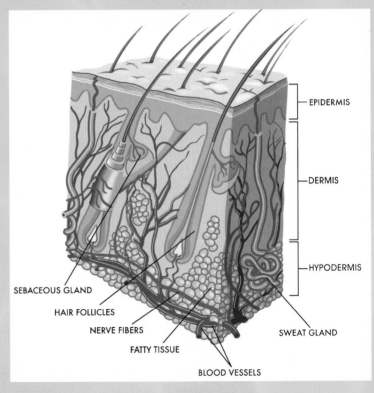

The structure of human skin

Our skin has many functions:

🦠 It is a barrier. The tightly packed cells containing keratin prevent entry of microbes. Sweat and oil keep microbes from spending time on the skin. As old cells constantly flake off they take microbes with them.

🦠 When sunlight hits the epidermis, vitamin D is made. Vitamin D is needed for healthy bones.

🦠 The many nerves in the skin make it a sensory organ. It helps us gather information about the outside world. For example, some nerve cells tell our brain when we are too hot. The brain then sends signals to increase blood flow at the skin's surface. This releases heat. If we are cold the opposite occurs.

🦠 The skin also has holes. For our eyes, nose, ears, and mouth to work properly they can't be covered by a thick layer of skin! At the same time we can't have undefended doorways into our bodies. There have to be other barriers. For example, our eyes have a thick protective membrane called the conjunctiva. It covers the inside of our eyelid and the eyeball. Our tear glands also produce tears that constantly flush microbes and dirt out of our eyes. Tears also contain enzymes that can kill microbes.

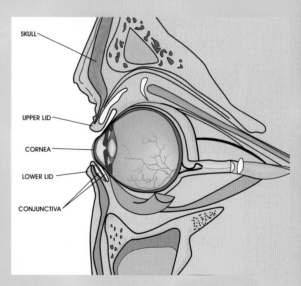

The structure of the human eye

Chapter 1

THE CASE OF
the Flesh-Eating Bacteria

The Crime

Fourteen-year-old Allison went on a weeklong camping trip with her family. She was allowed to take several friends with her. They arrived late Friday night. Allison and her friends rose bright and early for fun on Saturday. Before the week ended, though, Allison was in the intensive care unit of a hospital.

The Clues

When I met Allison at the emergency room on Thursday, I collected the following case history:

On Saturday, Allison and her friends explored a cave. At dinner her mother noticed Allison had a scrape on her left arm. Allison did not remember hurting her arm. To her it was no big deal and she forgot

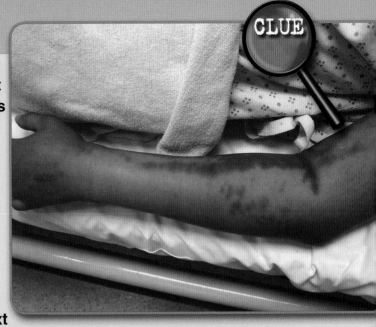

about it. That evening Allison felt like she had the flu. First she was cold and then she was hot. She had a headache. She felt sore all over. Surprisingly, the next morning, Allison felt fine. She and her friends rode horses all day. The next day, they all went on a canoe ride.

On Tuesday, Allison's lower left arm really hurt. She thought it was from canoeing. On the next day, the pain in Allison's arm was horrible. Later that afternoon she felt very sick again, just like she had on Saturday night. She was very weak, and alternated between cold and hot. She was up the entire night with vomiting and diarrhea.

Because Allison was so ill, her parents decided the trip was over and returned home. I got the call when they arrived at the emergency room (ER). The ER doctors treating Allison were concerned. Her blood pressure was very low. Her heartbeat was rapid. She was also dehydrated. When I examined her arm this is what I saw:

✳ There was a small scrape on the left arm.

✳ The lower arm was very swollen, red, and hot.

✳ The lower arm was extremely painful to Allison. It was more painful than it should have been.

Late Thursday night Allison's body gave out and she had to be taken to the intensive care unit. She was unconscious for the next twelve days.

Allison's arm being swollen, red, and hot indicated an infection. But what culprit had infected her? I had no clues to point me to a specific microbe. I decided to concentrate on how to get Allison better. I feared this was not a misdemeanor infection because:

- The flu symptoms she experienced when she first got the scrape and then again four days later are very serious symptoms.

- The pain she felt was so much more than what would be expected for that amount of swelling.

- Her low blood pressure, rapid heartbeat, high fever, and dehydration meant her whole body had been pulled into this health battle.

- The only visible injury on her arm was very minor considering the degree of her symptoms.

Based on these clues I suspected Allison was suffering from necrotizing fasciitis (NF). This disease moves very fast and is very destructive. In the 1990s, attacks by this disease were all over the newspapers and television. The media named the criminals "flesh-eating bacteria."

One bacterial thug that is often associated with NF is Group A *Streptococcus* (GAS). It also causes strep throat. These guys may use heavy enzymatic weapons that quickly destroy tissue. However, disease investigators raiding NF wounds have identified many types of bacterial gangsters, not just GAS bacteria. NF now seems to be some type of multi-microbial attack.

The death rate in NF cases is very high. Allison was getting weaker by the hour. I needed to verify if Allison had NF.

Magnetic Resonance Imaging (MRI) of Allison's Arm

In an MRI the body is exposed to a strong magnetic field. The magnetic energy makes atoms in the body spin. A computer is able to take the information from the spinning atoms and translate it into a highly detailed picture of the body.

Result: Allison's MRI showed a detailed picture of how deep this infection had gone into her arm. It also showed that gas was accumulating. There were definite signs that the tissue in Allison's arm was dying.

The Finger Test

Allison was still unconscious. In a sterile operating room I made a small but deep cut in the tissue of her arm. I then observed what leaked out of the arm. I next used my finger to examine the tissue of Allison's wound.

Result: When I cut Allison's arm, liquid the color of dirty dishwater leaked out. This was a clear sign of NF. When I probed the deep tissue of Allison's arm it was very soft and squishy. It should have been firm.

Allison had necrotizing fasciitis, but who did it?

These two tests supported my theory that Allison had NF. Many cases of NF involve multiple microbial attackers. Because NF kills fast, there was no time to find and charge a specific bacterial criminal with this crime. To save Allison's life <u>ALL</u> microbes in the affected area were sentenced to be eliminated.

Justice

Allison needed four surgeries. Each one removed more decaying tissue that contained the microbial trespassers from her arm. During this time, Allison was also given huge amounts of antibiotics to fight off these bacteria. During the first surgery, a sample was taken from the edge of the damaged tissue. This sample was tested in the laboratory. Group A *Streptococcus* was indeed present, but so were many other bacteria.

Twelve days after she passed out, Allison woke up. She had lost a lot of tissue from her arm. But she was on the mend. I never identified all the culprits in this case. But the important thing was that Allison was alive and still had her arm.

Antibiotics and surgeries cured Allison.

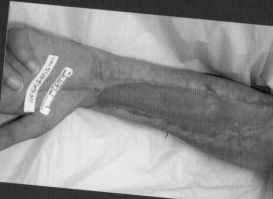

Allison's healing arm

Protect Yourself

NF attacks are sudden and unexpected. But there are some things you can do to prevent NF.

- Any break in your skin is a danger, no matter how small it may be. Care for all skin injuries by keeping them clean and applying antibiotic ointment.

- Group A *Streptococcus* is a prime suspect in NF attacks. These guys will also be present in the throats of people with strep throat. This means that people with strep throat need to be extra cautious around other people. The microbial offenders in their throats could end up causing NF in someone else, or in themselves.

- Remember: If an area is swollen, red, hot, and painful, you may have an infection. If you have an infection that accompanies flu-like symptoms, make sure you see a doctor.

This is Agent Annie Biotica signing off. Stay safe out there.

Chapter 2

Pinkeye and THE CASE OF the Sticky Penny

The Crime

A five-year-old boy named Lacika was at kindergarten one day. He saw a penny on the playground. When he picked it up it was gross and sticky. Lacika dropped the penny back into the dirt. As he waited in line to go back inside the school he rubbed his eye. That was a big mistake. The next day he woke up and couldn't open his eye! It was glued shut with yellow crusty stuff. His mother had to pull his eye open. Then she saw that the white part of the eyeball was all red. That is when I got the call.

The Clues

I met Lacika and his mother at their doctor's office. These were his symptoms:

- Thick yellow goo was oozing from his eye.
- The eye was swollen and sore.
- The eye was bloodshot.
- The lining inside the lower eyelid was bright red.

The Suspects

It seemed pretty obvious that Lacika had an infection of the conjunctiva. This is a thin membrane that lines the inside of the eyelid and the eyeball. The disease is called conjunctivitis. This microbial attack causes the blood vessels in the eye to swell. This is why conjunctivitis is often called "pinkeye."

Eye infections can be caused by both bacteria and viruses. If this was a bacterial attack there were three suspects. Many pinkeye crimes are committed by members of *Haemophilus*, *Streptococcus*, or *Staphylococcus* gangs. If the attack was

Iris Pupil Sclera

Conjunctiva (lines eyelids and surface of eye)

viral then the criminal adenovirus would be my prime suspect. This bad guy will hit anyone if given the chance, but he is notorious for attacking little kids. Adenoviruses spread easily. They have infected entire schools. My job was to find out if this was a viral or bacterial attack. I compared the symptoms.

Both viruses and bacteria can cause pinkeye.

Lacika's Symptoms	Bacterial Pinkeye	Viral Pinkeye
Thick yellow discharge	Yes	No
Eye swollen	Yes	Yes
Eye bloodshot	Yes	Yes
Conjunctiva bright red	Yes	Yes

The clues leaned toward a bacterial attack. There were also three symptoms of viral pinkeye that Lacika did not have.

1. He did not feel like there was dirt in his eye.

2. His eye was not horribly painful.

3. He had not had a recent respiratory infection.

These are almost always seen in viral eye attacks. No, I was pretty sure Lacika had bacterial conjunctivitis. But to get a conviction, I needed proof. The three bacterial gangs I needed to question were the *Haemophilus*, *Streptococcus*, and *Staphylococcus* gangs.

SUSPECT #1 – THE *HAEMOPHILUS* GANG

SUSPECT #2 – THE *STREPTOCOCCUS* GANG

SUSPECT #3 – THE *STAPHYLOCOCCUS* GANG

The Case of the Flesh-Eating Bacteria

A Gram stain is a laboratory test that divides all the bacteria in the world into two groups. If they stain purple they are gram-positive. If they stain pink they are gram-negative. Staining also helps me see the shape and size of the bacteria. I gently collected some of the yellow ooze from Lacika's eye. I smeared the ooze onto a microscope slide. Then I did the test.

Gram Stain the Bacteria

Result: The Gram stain test was positive for *Streptococcus* type bacteria.
    Under the microscope I saw a lot of purple (gram-positive) round bacterial cells that were in chains. *Haemophilus* bacteria would have been pink, gram-negative, and very small rods. *Staphylococcus* bacteria would have been gram-positive and round, but in bunches like grapes. This was good evidence. However, it is always best to have two positive IDs.

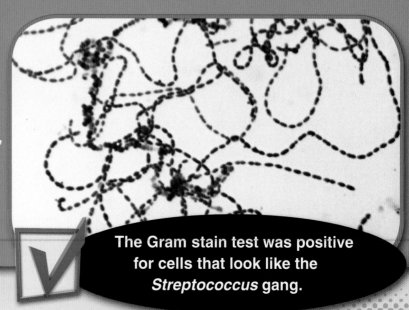

The Gram stain test was positive for cells that look like the *Streptococcus* gang.

Quick Test for *Streptococcus pneumoniae*

The one member of the *Streptococcus* gang that is famous for pinkeye crimes is *Streptococcus pneumoniae.* This guy is such a health menace that companies have made easy rapid strep tests to identify it in victims.

To perform the rapid strep test, I needed a larger sample of the bacteria that was attacking Lacika's eye. I used a cotton swab to take another sample. Then I rubbed the swab over the surface of a petri dish that contained agar. A petri dish is a small plastic dish with a lid. Agar is a mixture of sugars and red algae harvested from places like Asia and California. It feels like a firm jelly. This gives the microbes a place to sit

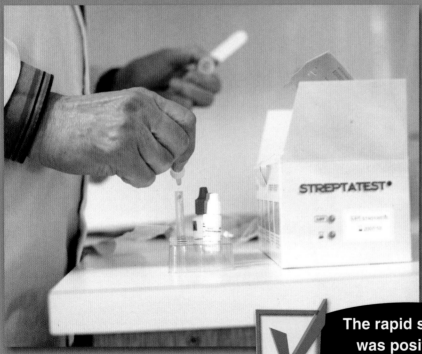

and food to eat. After twenty-four hours, enough bacteria had grown to perform the rapid test.

Result: The rapid test for *S. pneumoniae* was positive.

The rapid strep test was positive for Lacika's sample.

The Verdict

The bacteria *S. pneumoniae* was found guilty on all counts of this eye attack and sentenced to be eliminated.

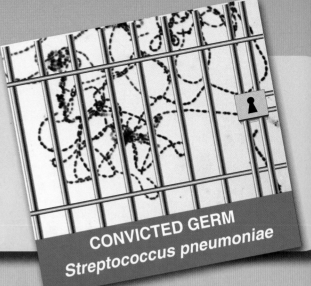

CONVICTED GERM
Streptococcus pneumoniae

Justice

Lacika was given eye drops containing a strong antibiotic. Because Lacika's eye was leaking bacteria he could pass the criminals to other people. I cautioned Lacika that he should avoid touching his eyes. He should wash his hands often and throw away all used tissues. Lacika's school recommended that he stay home until he had been on antibiotics for a few days.

Protect Yourself

It is never a good idea to rub your eyes. Hands often contain microbial criminals, so you may be helping diseases enter your body if you rub your eyes. Also, the rubbing action can physically damage your eye.

This is Agent Annie Biotica signing off. Stay safe out there.

Chapter 3

Ringworm and THE CASE OF the Ugly Toenails

The Crime

It was Josya's birthday and she really wanted a pedicure. She took her birthday money and went to a local beauty salon that was advertising a special. Josya was so excited when she sat down in the pedicure chair. First, the salon worker picked a nail file from a plastic box beside the pedicure chair. After filing Josya's toenails she tossed the nail file back into the plastic box. The salon girl picked up a foot bath full of water. She dumped it out in the sink and refilled it. Josya soaked her feet for ten minutes. Next the salon girl took a wooden stick from the plastic box. She scraped all around and underneath Josya's toenails.

The wooden stick was returned to the plastic box. When the pedicure was over Josya left the salon happy with newly painted toenails.

A week later Josya removed the nail polish from her toes. She noticed some yellow spots on some of her toenails. Unfortunately, this was only the beginning of Josya's toenail problem.

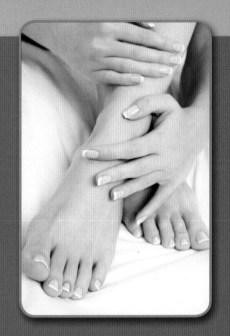

Josya had a pedicure for her birthday.

The Clues

When I was assigned to Josya's case I met her at a foot doctor's office. Two of her toenails were in bad shape. These were her symptoms:

- The affected toenails had become very thick.
- They were brittle and ragged.
- They had turned a chalky white with yellow and dark areas.
- Parts of the nails were coming loose from her toe.

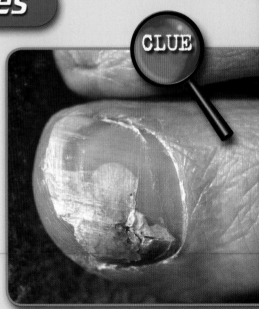

CLUE

After hearing about Josya's unpleasant pedicure, I had a hunch. My gut was telling me that Josya had been attacked by a fungus. Doctors use the word *tinea* for fungal health crimes. Tinea attacks are committed by a tricky fungal gang called dermatophytes. These guys will attack just about anywhere on the body. When they go after the skin they leave big circles of rashes (tinea corporis). When they wage war on the scalp, a person's hair falls out (tinea capitis). They are also the ones that cause athlete's foot (tinea pedis). These attacks are also called "ringworm" because people once thought a worm was the culprit. Poor Josya had tinea unguium. This is ringworm of the nails. Seeing Josya cry made me see red. I decided to visit that beauty salon.

I questioned the owner of the salon where Josya had her pedicure. I found out the salon did not sterilize or use new tools for each client. They also didn't bother to disinfect the footbaths in between clients. The owner felt these precautions unnecessary. At one point a salon employee motioned to me. We spoke in private in the parking lot. She told me that a woman with suspicious-looking toenails had gotten a pedicure the same day as Josya. I could imagine the dermatophytes hanging onto the pedicure tools and hiding out in the footbath waiting for a new victim. When I left the salon I took their pedicure tools and footbath with me. It was time to close this case.

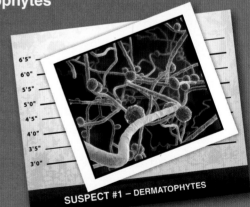

SUSPECT #1 – DERMATOPHYTES

I carefully scraped the skin around Josya's infected toenails using a sterile tool. I placed the scrapings on a microscope slide. On a second slide I put a sample taken from the wooden pedicure tool that I had taken from the beauty parlor. I examined the slides under a microscope.

Microscopic Examination

Result: Both samples were positive for typical fungal cells. This test showed that Josya had a fungal infection of her toenails. It also showed that the tools taken from the beauty parlor were contaminated with fungus. For a more positive identification, I did a second test.

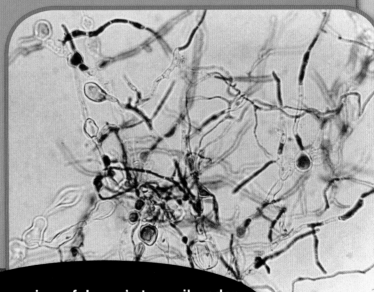

A scraping of Josya's toenail under the microscope

Test Two

Grow the Fungus

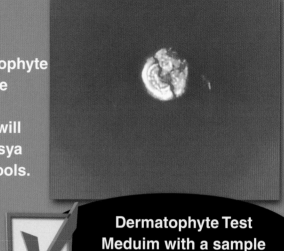

I used a special agar called Dermatophyte Test Medium (DTM). It is specially made to grow and identify dermatophytes. If dermatophytes are present the media will turn red. I took new scrapings from Josya and also a sample from the pedicure tools. I placed each test sample on a petri dish with DTM. I allowed the samples to sit in the dish for ten days.

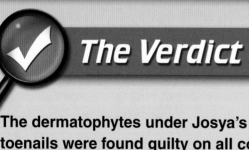

Dermatophyte Test Meduim with a sample from Josya's toenail

Result: Both samples were positive for dermatophytes.

After ten days fungus had grown on both plates. Also, the media around each sample had turned red. This test proved beyond a reasonable doubt that Josya had been attacked by the dermatophytes. It was also strong evidence that the pedicure tools were the source of her attack.

The Verdict

The dermatophytes under Josya's toenails were found guilty on all counts. They were sentenced to be eliminated. The owner of the beauty salon was also charged and found guilty of endangering the public's health.

CONVICTED GERM
Dermatophytes

Justice

Dermatophytes are tough. Once they stake out a territory they hang on. Over-the-counter fungal treatments were not strong enough to stop Josya's attack. She had to take a prescription antifungal medicine by mouth. The dermatophytes fought back with everything they had. Josya took her medicine for three months before her toenails began to heal. She also had to keep a lookout for a second attack. A toenail attack like this is not cured until a new toenail has grown in.

Protect Yourself

These are some things you can do to have a healthy trip to a spa or salon:

- Make sure employees always wash their hands before beginning a service.
- If you are getting a manicure you should wash your hands first or use an alcohol-based sanitizer.
- Make sure that items that were used on another client have been cleaned and disinfected.
- Some items should be thrown away after use. These include foam files, emery boards, foam buffers, toe separators, and tools for applying lotion or makeup.
- Do not shave your legs for at least twenty-four hours before having a pedicure. Tiny cuts in the skin can let in microbes.
- Ask if your footbath has been cleaned and disinfected. The footbath should be filled with water immediately before you use it.

Chapter 4

Chicken Pox
and THE CASE OF
the Tangled Web of Infections

The Crime

One of my arch germ enemies is the varicella zoster virus, nicknamed VZV. This germ criminal is very smart. Once inside a person's body it never leaves. It is also able to cause two different diseases! It floats in the air and enters through the nose or mouth. But it is the skin it is really after. Its first attack on a person causes the disease known as chicken pox. VZV then hides out in the nerves around the spinal cord. When it decides to cause more trouble, it wakes up and crawls back to the skin. When VZV launches later attacks it causes a disease called shingles. VZV loves to travel so it is very contagious. One of the most confusing cases of my career involved a young family attacked by VZV.

Chicken Pox

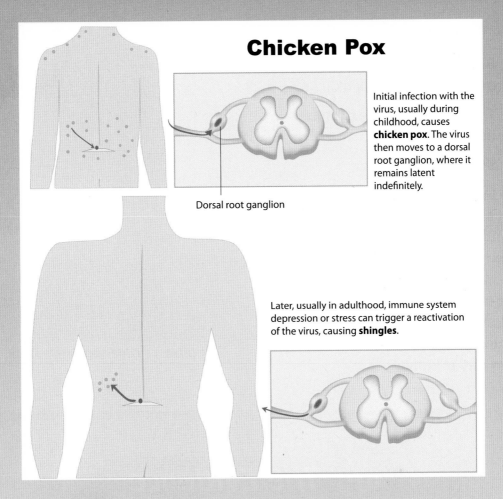

Initial infection with the virus, usually during childhood, causes **chicken pox**. The virus then moves to a dorsal root ganglion, where it remains latent indefinitely.

Dorsal root ganglion

Later, usually in adulthood, immune system depression or stress can trigger a reactivation of the virus, causing **shingles**.

Attack Number One

One day I was called to a hospital to help a young pregnant mother. Erin's husband was away in the military. She was home alone with their young daughter. Now she had been attacked by some microbe criminal. Her baby boy was soon to be born and she feared for his health. Let's look at her symptoms on the next page.

- She had fluid-filled blisters on her chest and back.
- The blisters were extremely itchy.
- She had a low fever.

The look of the blisters on Erin's back made them easy to identify. Erin had chicken pox. When I questioned her she said she had never had the disease as a child. Erin didn't believe that she had chicken pox. She wanted proof before she would allow any treatment.

The blisters covering Erin's back

The Evidence

I took a sample of Erin's blood and tested it for antibodies against VZV. Antibodies are Y-shaped proteins made by the body's immune system. Each antibody is made to recognize only one microbial invader.

Result: Erin's blood had antibodies that matched the VZV. This means that her body had been invaded by VZV.

The Verdict

Based on the unique look of the blisters and a positive antibody test, VZV was found guilty of attacking Erin.

CONVICTED GERM
VZV

Justice

Erin will only get partial justice. Because VZV will hide in Erin's nerve cells she will always be infected. While most childhood chicken pox attacks are not deadly, adult ones often are. Death usually occurs from complications like pneumonia (severe lung infection) and encephalitis (brain swelling). Erin was given antiviral medicines. She was also given antibodies taken from other people infected with VZV. Both of these treatments would help reduce the amount of VZV in her body. My hope was that they wouldn't attack her baby. I also cautioned Erin against scratching the itchy blisters. That could lead to infection and scarring.

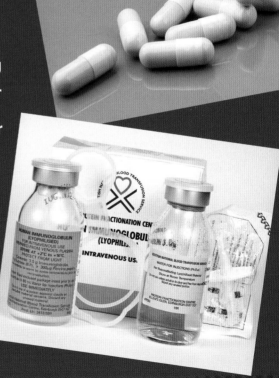

Antiviral medicine and antibodies helped contain Erin's VZV infection.

Attack Number Two

Baby boy Cullen was born a week after Erin began antiviral treatment. To protect Cullen I told Erin to always keep the affected skin covered. Once the blisters crusted over and healed they would no longer be contagious.

I was called back on this case when Cullen was eight months old. At the hospital Cullen was cooing happily. Erin had brought him in because he had some fluid filled blisters on his back and one arm. They had been there several days. Erin feared Cullen might have caught chicken pox from her. But how? She had been very careful not to let her blisters touch him. Also, her blisters had healed months ago. He had only had his for several days.

I noticed right away that Cullen's blisters were different from Erin's.

 They were clumped together in groups.

 They were only on the left side of his back and his left arm.

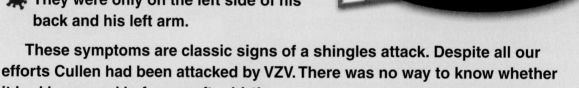

Cullen's PCR test was positive for VZV.

These symptoms are classic signs of a shingles attack. Despite all our efforts Cullen had been attacked by VZV. There was no way to know whether it had happened before or after birth.

Erin was confused. Cullen had never showed signs of chicken pox. How could he now have shingles? I explained that when she had been treated with antiviral medicine and anti-VZV antibodies, so had Cullen. They had shared blood before he was born. Afterward he had gotten them from her through breast milk. These treatments had not been enough to prevent the VZV attack. But they had allowed Cullen to have extremely mild chicken pox symptoms. So mild they had gone unnoticed. But why did he now have shingles?

Erin had stopped breast-feeding Cullen two months ago. Now that Cullen was no longer receiving protection, VZV had launched a second attack. One third of babies attacked by VZV before or soon after birth develop shingles before they are five. Erin wanted to believe me but she needed proof. After all, babies do get lots of rashes.

Test #1 Test Cullen for VZV

I took a small sample of fluid from Cullen's blisters. I used the fluid in a polymerase chain reaction (PCR) test. PCR uses small guided missiles called primers. The primers search out the genetic material inside VZV. The primers are very sensitive so they can detect very tiny amounts of virus. The primers are very specific so they will only attach to VZV.

Result: Cullen's blister fluid was positive for VZV.

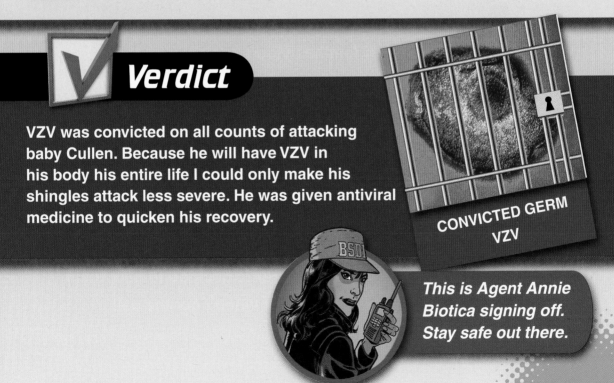

Verdict

VZV was convicted on all counts of attacking baby Cullen. Because he will have VZV in his body his entire life I could only make his shingles attack less severe. He was given antiviral medicine to quicken his recovery.

CONVICTED GERM
VZV

This is Agent Annie Biotica signing off. Stay safe out there.

Chapter 5

Measles and THE CASE OF the Stowaway Rash

The Crime

The Alvarez family was so excited. They were waiting at the airport for their adopted little girl to arrive. She was two years old and they had decided to name her Rosie. The Alvarezes were not alone. Nine other families stood happily with them. All ten families had adopted children from the same orphanage. It was a very happy day.

The Alvarezes had made arrangements for Rosie to see a pediatrician the day after she arrived. It was a good thing, too. Rosie seemed to be sick. She had a slight fever, a runny nose, a cough, and red throat. The doctor decided Rosie had a cold.

Five days later Rosie was even sicker. Seven of the other adopted children were also ill. The parents decided to take them all to the same emergency room. That's when I got the call.

The Clues

I started my investigation by examining all eight children. I found that their symptoms were almost identical. Shortly after arriving in this country they all had:

 Slight fever

 Cough

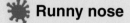 Runny nose

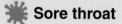 Sore throat

CLUE #1

Two days later:

Tiny white spots appeared in their mouths.

They all had high fevers.

During the next day or two:

A reddish-purple rash appeared on their faces. It seemed to be spreading toward their necks and chests. As time went on, the rash went all the way to their toes.

Those tiny white spots in the mouth and the rash were very interesting clues. I was pretty sure who the attacker was.

The white spots inside the children's mouths

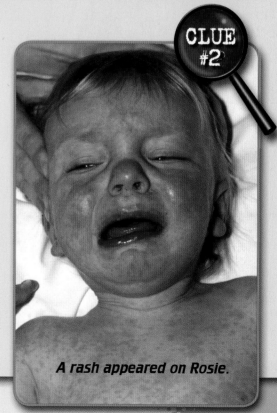

CLUE #2

A rash appeared on Rosie.

The Suspect

I believed these children had met up with a viral villain named measles. Measles is actually a scrawny little weakling. It can't survive one minute in the world on its own. It is always on the lookout for a nose or mouth to enter. A vaccine against this virus was developed in 1963. It has been very successful in the United States. Before vaccination almost 4 million people were attacked each year. Of these victims, 500 usually died. It was important to help these kids quickly.

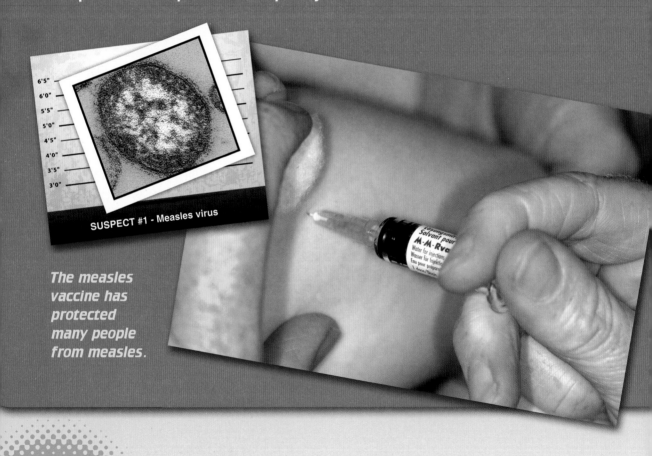

SUSPECT #1 - Measles virus

The measles vaccine has protected many people from measles.

The Evidence

A lot of microbe criminals cause cold symptoms and a rash. Was this really measles?

I took a sample of blood from all of the children. I tested each for antibodies. These are Y-shaped proteins the body's immune system makes while fighting a microbial attacker. If these children had measles then their bodies would have made antibodies against the virus.

 ## Test Blood for Antibodies

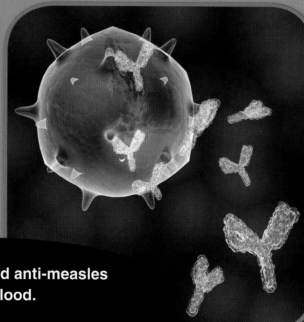

Result: All samples were positive for measles antibodies.

This is very strong evidence that these children had been violated by measles. However, to get a conviction I needed to be sure.

 All eight children had anti-measles antibodies in their blood.

Test Two

Test for the Virus

I went back to the children the next day. I used a sterile cotton swab to rub the children's throats. I then performed the polymerase chain reaction (PCR) test. PCR uses small guided missiles called primers. The primers act as bloodhounds seeking out their target.

Result: All eight throat swabs were positive for the measles virus.

All eight children had the measles virus in their bodies.

The Verdict

The measles virus was found guilty on all counts of attacking the adopted children.

CONVICTED GERM
Measles virus

The Case of the Flesh-Eating Bacteria

Justice

Unfortunately, there is no cure for measles. The only way to help the victims is to watch them carefully. Many times measles is not satisfied with causing discomfort and a rash. Sometimes it goes after the lungs and causes pneumonia. Other times it goes after the brain and causes swelling and brain damage. If there is evidence either of these is occurring, doctors can try medicines to minimize the damage. For this reason, all the children were kept in the hospital until they were well again.

Foreign Invader

I was concerned. How did measles get to these kids? After continuing to work this case I figured it out. Rosie and the seven other children got their rashes within five days of being in the United States. It takes eleven days for the measles virus to cause the rash. These eight children all came from the same orphanage. That must have been the site of the attacks.

Protect Yourself

Many people today have forgotten that measles still lurks around. The United States fought measles hard with a vaccine. However, measles is still common in many countries. Keep this in mind if you travel to a foreign country. If you haven't been vaccinated, then you are at risk.

This is Agent Annie Biotica signing off. Stay safe out there.

You Solve the Case

Twleve-year-old Kourtney went to the mall with her friends. They went shoe shopping. Kourtney found a pair of shoes she loved.

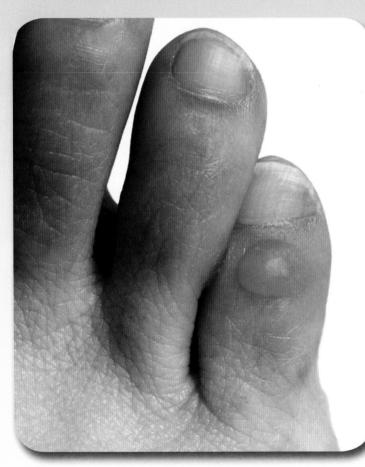

Unfortunately they were a little tight on her feet. They were just so cool that she decided to buy them anyway. After wearing the shoes to school she got a blister on her little toe. She stopped wearing the shoes but the blister did not heal. The wound started to ooze a yellow fluid that smelled awful. Kourtney's mother applied an over-the-counter antibiotic ointment to her daughter's toe. This did not seem to help. Two days later Kourtney's mother took her to the emergency room.

Kourtney's problem first started with a blishter on her toe.

The Case of the Flesh-Eating Bacteria

✳ Her toe was very swollen, red, hot, and painful. Do you think Kourtney's toe was infected?

✳ At the ER an MRI was done on Kourtney's toe. It did not show signs of gas production or large scale tissue destruction. Do these clues support a diagnosis of necrotizing fasciitis (NF)?

✳ Kourtney's toe hurt, she was not running a fever, and she did not experience any flu-like symptoms. Do these clues support a diagnosis of necrotizing fasciitis (NF)?

You Solve the Case

Sonja was a very healthy and active sixty-two-year-old woman. She swam every day and loved to garden. One weekend Sonja started to feel ill. For three days she felt tired, had a headache, and was a little nauseated. By Tuesday Sonja noticed some red spots near her belly button. There was also a tingling feeling at the site of the red spots. By Friday there were more areas of red spots. The red spots kept

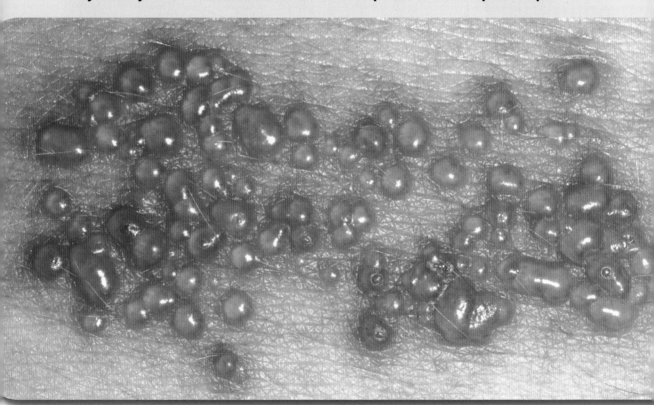

The first group of blisters on Sonja's stomach

coming in clumps. As more clumps appeared they started to blend together into a huge red rash. Each clump started as just red spots but then became fluid-filled blisters. When the blisters broke open they left painful sores.

After only a week a band of rash and blisters had wrapped around one side of Sonja's body. It started at the right side of her belly button and reached around to her backbone. What was even worse was that the tingling feeling in those spots had turned into pain. The pain was so horrible Sonja couldn't stand to have anything touch her skin. She wasn't even able to sleep. Sonja went to her doctor. The doctor asked her two questions.

1. Had Sonja ever had chicken pox? Sonja said yes.

2. On a scale of one to ten, how much do the clumps of blisters hurt? Sonja answered twenty!

The doctor prescribed antiviral medicine and painkillers. Sonja was sick and in terrible pain for three whole months. Eventually, the blisters healed and the pain went away.

What disease did Sonja have?

You Solve the Case

CASE #3

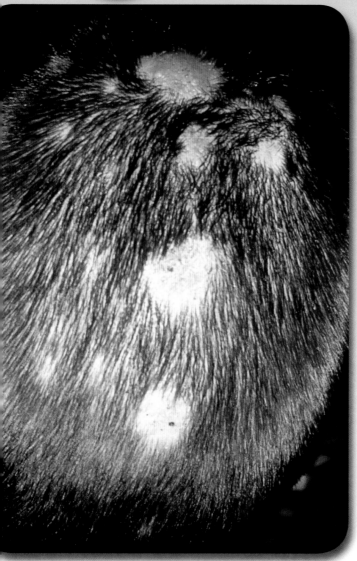

Mario's head when he went to the doctor

Mario was so excited. He was going to summer camp this year! Mario was gone for two whole weeks. When he got home he had lots of stories to tell. All day his mother would hear about the seven other boys Mario shared a cabin with. His favorite story was about how they would switch beds each night as a game.

As Mario's mother was listening to this story she noticed Mario's hair looked oily and dirty. She asked if he had stopped washing his hair. Mario looked a little embarrassed and said that he had not been shampooing

The Case of the Flesh-Eating Bacteria

his hair. He said his head was sore and it hurt to rub it. Mario's mother looked at his head more closely. She noticed quite a few round spots on his scalp that looked odd. She took Mario to the barbershop and got his hair cut short. Now she saw obvious bald spots on Mario's head. The skin within each circle looked red and dry. She thought that maybe he had become allergic to the shampoo they were using.

Changing shampoos didn't seem to help. Mario said his head still hurt and the bald, red circles were getting larger. It was time to see a doctor. The doctor first examined Mario's head carefully. Then he scraped some skin from one of the bald spots. He examined the skin sample under a microscope. He told Mario's mother that Mario had dermatophytes growing on his scalp.

What was wrong with Mario's head?

You Solve the Case: The Answers

CASE #1 — Infection

These four signs indicate an infection. Do these clues support a diagnosis of necrotizing fasciitis (NF)? No.

Kourtney's toe hurt, but not horribly. She had no fever and did not experience any flu-like symptoms. Kourtney seems to have had a small infection. Her skin broke open from getting a blister. This allowed bacteria to enter and multiply, causing an infection. However, these bacteria were not bad enough to cause NF. It is possible the infection was too advanced for the antibiotic ointment to help. It is also possible that the tube Kourtney's mother used had expired.

CASE #2 — Shingles

Sonja had shingles. Shingles is a disease that occurs in people who have been infected with the varicella zoster virus. The first time someone is infected with this virus they get the disease chicken pox. Then the virus hides out inside the body. This virus can come out of hiding and attack again, causing shingles.

CASE #3 — Tinea Capitis

Mario had tinea capitis, also called ringworm of the scalp. The doctor explained that it is often called ringworm because it leaves circular marks. It is not caused by a worm at all. It is a fungal infection of the scalp. The fungal cells are called dermatophytes. Mario's mother asked the doctor if he could have gotten this by sleeping in other people's beds. The doctor said yes. If one of the boys at camp had scalp ringworm then his pillow would have been contaminated. He also could have gotten infected from direct contact with an infected person's head, for example if they were wrestling. Dermatophytes are very contagious.

Glossary

agar: A gelatin substance high in sugar and made from red algae. It gives bacteria a place to grow and food to eat.

antibiotics: Medicines that inhibit the growth of bacteria.

antibodies: Y-shaped proteins made by the body that help fight off invaders.

conjunctiva: The tissue that lines the eyeball and the inside of the eyelid.

dermatophyte: A type of fungus that grows underneath fingernails and toenails and elsewhere.

Dermatophyte Test Medium (DTM): A special growth medium for culturing fungus.

dermis: The deepest layer of the skin.

encephalitis: A swelling of the brain.

epidermis: The top layer of the skin.

fungus: Microscopic organism whose structure can resemble that of a plant.

Gram stain: A chemical test that identifies a bacterium as being from one of two groups.

hypodermis: The layer of tissue that connects the skin to the body.

keratin: A protein that builds up in skin cells. It makes cells stronger and waterproof.

Magnetic Resonance Imaging (MRI): A medical test that gives very detailed pictures of the inside of the body.

PCR primers: Small pieces of RNA or DNA that find and stick to the genetic material of a microbe.

Glossary

pinkeye: An infection of the eye that can be bacterial or viral. If the conjunctiva of the eye is affected it is also called conjunctivitis.

pneumonia: A disease that results from microbes invading the lungs.

polymerase chain reaction (PCR): A laboratory test that can detect the genetic material in a microbe.

sebaceous glands: The glands in skin that make oil.

vaccine: Usually a shot. It gives a person a harmless version of a microbe so that the immune system can begin working on ways to protect itself.

Further Reading

Glaser, Jason. *Pinkeye.* Mankato, Minn.: Capstone Press, 2006.

Klosterman, Lorrie. *Skin.* New York: Marshall Cavendish Benchmark, 2009.

Landau, Elaine. *Chickenpox.* New York: Marshall Cavendish Benchmark, 2010.

Levy, Janey. *The World of Microbes: Bacteria, Viruses, and Other Microorganisms.* New York: Rosen, 2011.

Tilden, Thomasine E. Lewis. *Help! What's Eating My Flesh?: Runaway Staph and Strep Infections!* New York: Franklin Watts, 2008.

Internet Addresses

Centers for Disease Control and Prevention. "Conjunctivitis (Pink Eye)."
<http://www.cdc.gov/conjunctivitis/index.html>

The National Necrotizing Fasciitis Foundation.
<http://www.nnff.org>

Index

A
adenovirus, 16
agar, 18
antibiotics, 12, 13, 19, 39
antibodies, 28, 29, 30, 35,

C
chicken pox. *See* varicella zoster virus
collagen, 6
conjunctiva, 7, 15
conjunctivitis, 15

D
dermis, 6
dermatophyte, 22, 24, 25, 43, 44
Dermatophyte Test Medium (DTM), 24

E
elastin, 6
encephalitis, 29
epidermis, 6

F
flesh-eating bacteria, 10

G
Gram stains, 17

H
Haemophilus, 15, 16, 17

K
keratin, 6

M
magnetic resonance imaging (MRI), 11, 39
measles, 34, 35, 36

N
necrotizing fasciitis (NF), 10, 11, 12, 13, 39, 44
nerves, 7

P
pinkeye. *See* conjunctivitis
pneumonia, 29, 37
polymerase chain reaction (PCR) test, 31, 36

R
rapid strep test, 18
ringworm. *See* tinea

S
sebaceous glands, 6

shingles. *See* varicella zoster virus
skin
    functions, 7
    layers, 6
Staphylococcus, 15, 16, 17
Streptococcus, 15, 16, 17
    Group A *Streptococcus* (GAS), 10, 12, 13
    Streptococcus pneumoniae, 18, 19

T
tinea, 22
    tinea capitis, 22, 44
    tinea corporis, 22
    tinea pedis, 22

V
varicella zoster virus (VZV), 26, 28, 29, 30-31, 41, 44
vitamin D, 7